AN
ACTOR'S
CAROL

Charles Evered

BROADWAY PLAY PUBLISHING INC
New York
www.broadwayplaypub.com
info@broadwayplaypub.com

Cover art by Jacqueline Gaul

First edition: March 2019
I S B N: 978-0-88145-827-5

Book design: Marie Donovan
Page make-up: Adobe InDesign
Typeface: Palatino

Dedicated to the memory of my beautiful sister,
Kathleen Evered

AN ACTOR'S CAROL was developed over a period of four years with the productions and presentations listed as follows. Each helped advance the script, for which I am very thankful.

AN ACTOR'S CAROL had its world premiere in December 2015 at the Hi-Desert Cultural Center, Joshua Tree, California. The cast and creative contributors were:

HUGH PENDLETON .... Hal Linden/Barry Cutler
Player 1 .... Noelle Geiger
Player 2 .... Kirk Geiger
Player 3 .... Ben Atkinson

Director .... Charles Evered
Sets .... Amy Angel
Technical director .... Matthew Garrett

Special thanks to Alexis Dickey *for her participation as Player 1 in the script workshop process.*

AN ACTOR'S CAROL was presented as a staged reading in December 2016 at the Arts Council of Princeton, Princeton, New Jersey. The cast and creative contributors were:

HUGH PENDLETON .... Morgan Murphy
Player 1 .... Wendy Rolfe Evered
Player 2 .... Drew Militano
Player 3 .... Frank Favata

Director .... Morgan Murphy

AN ACTOR'S CAROL was presented as a benefit staged reading for the Charles J Evered House in December 2017 at the Melissa Morgan Gallery, Palm Desert, California. The cast and creative contributors were:

HUGH PENDLETON .... Miles Anderson
Player 1 .... Wendy Rolfe Evered
Player 2 .... Kirk Geiger
Player 3 .... Marty James

Director .... Noelle Geiger

AN ACTOR'S CAROL had its New Jersey premiere in December 2018 at Cape May Stage, Cape May, New Jersey. The cast and creative contributors were:

HUGH PENDLETON .... John Little
Player 1 .... Kirsten Hopkins
Player 2 .... Kevin Cristaldi
Player 3 .... Karack Osborn

Director .... Roy B Steinberg
Sets .... Spencer Potter
Lighting .... Heather Crocker
Costumes .... Sera Bourgeau
Stage manager .... Amy Hadam

AN ACTOR'S CAROL had its Washington State premiere in December 2018 by The Lesser-Known Players, Bainbridge Island. The cast and creative contributors were:

HUGH PENDLETON ....Nelsen Spickard
ensemble .... Bronsyn Beth Foster, Jennifer Hodges, Duncan Menzies, Michael C Moore, Geoff Schmidt, George Shannon, Tyler Weaver

Director .... Jennifer Hodges
Assistant director .... Karen Hauser
Lighting .... Jim Cash
Composer/Musical director .... Jon Brenner

NOTES

AN ACTOR'S CAROL can be produced by itself, or in repertory along with A CHRISTMAS CAROL.

It can be produced on and around an existing CHRISTMAS CAROL set.

One scenario might be to have the same actor play Scrooge in this play, that is playing him in a currently running production of A CHRISTMAS CAROL.

The play can be cast with *as few as four actors*, one female, or, it can be cast traditionally with seventeen actors.

There are purposefully timely and local references in the play, that local companies should feel free to change in order to make more personalized and fun.

The U C P should call out actual seat numbers when interacting with the audience.

The name of a local supermarket should be inserted.

The name of local theatre awards should be added to the "low life" scenes.

CHARACTERS & SETTING

HUGH PENDLETON, *an actor*

Player 1, female: TINA, KATE, SUSAN, S M C P, ACTOR 1, LOW LIFE 1

Player 2, male: George, U C P, C C Y C, Janitor

Player 3, male: DEREK, MARTY, BIRDY, JEFFREY, ACTOR 2, LOW LIFE 2.

Time: The present. Christmas Eve.

Place: A small, struggling theatre outside a big city.

Backstage, then onstage.

There is one intermission.

ACT ONE

(A minute or two before curtain, An USHER, *[our Usher], mixes in with the actual ushers from the theatre. Dressed in a red vest, hair askew and with a small flashlight hanging around his neck, he clearly stands out from the rest of the ushers. He's also missing a hand. Literally. The real ushers are kind of uncomfortable around him, confused. He's a little loud. A little pushy perhaps? He whistles, kind of berates the other ushers on how to hand out programs, etc. (Have fun, actor)* When the show's about to begin, he walks over and stands in front of or on the stage, takes out a small pile of index cards and clears his throat, very loudly. Trying to settle the audience down. When he does, he starts to read the following off separate 3 X 5 cards—as dryly as is humanly possible. Not a single smile. Dead pan. Arid, in fact.

USHER: *(Reading off card)* What did the usher say when he crossed the road? *(Quick pause)* "This way, please." *(Goes to next card)* Knock knock…

*(*USHER *encourages audience to say "who's there?")*

USHER: *(Cuts them off)* Quiet please. *(Pause)* What did the usher say when he took a librarian out to dinner? Nothing. He said absolutely nothing. In fact, they both just sat there in complete silence the whole night. Collegial respect, is what that's called. Oh and this is no joke, by the way, this actually happened to me.

(Starts to tear up, asks audience members) Anybody, have a tissue, seriously? Anybody?

(Hopefully he gets one—wipes eyes)

USHER: Yeah, she uh— kept thinking I was going to ask her to be "quiet please", and I kept thinking she was going to "shush" me. We didn't say a word to each other the whole magical night. We just sat there, looking into each other's eyes, lost in a fantasia of new-found love. Ended up marrying the lady. Thank you. Yeah, she uh—left me last week. For a mime. She said I was too "verbose". *(Puts cards away, clears throat again)* Anyway, truth be told, I come from a long line of ushers. My great great great grandfather Jebidiah was head usher at Ford's Theatre in Washington, DC. What? His first night of work was April 14th, 1865 what's so funny? *(Under his breath)* "Right this way, Mr Booth." Yeah, there have definitely been better first days of work.

Oh, before we begin: *(He can customize this a little, depending on venue)* Exits are over there. If something unexpected happens, it would be nice if you didn't trample the elderly on your way to saving your own butt. Thank you. There's two acts in this thing, so feel free to buy something to eat or drink at intermission. The money will go toward our exorbitant salaries. And finally, please turn off your cell phones and perhaps for one tiny second, stop being a slave to technology. Anywho, I've haunted you enough. Tata for now!

(USHER exits, with an over the top, ghoulish laugh as the Artistic Director or some REP from the actual theatre comes on stage, confused.)

THEATRE REP: Wait, who—who was that? Seriously, who was that?

(Here the THEATRE REP can finish the curtain speech, ending with something like the usual:)

THEATRE REP: Thank you for being here tonight, and please enjoy the show!

(The THEATRE REP *exits as lights fade to black.)*

(At rise: Where we find ourselves backstage, looking at the backside of a worn and distressed curtain. Near it, two basic playing areas, a makeup table, R, and a pile L, of various backstage articles: ropes, old drapes, etc. On the other side of the backdrop, we hear the faint sounds of a production of Dicken's "A Christmas Carol" in progress. We see some of the stage light spilling under the curtain.)

(We also notice, on his knees, with his somewhat sizeable backside prominently sticking out in our direction U C, a YOUNG MAN *with his head peeking through the middle of the curtain facing the unseen stage. He's listening intently. Suddenly, the sound of a cell phone ringing, backstage, muted. The Usher suddenly appears, looking out at the audience, incredulous:)*

USHER: Are you kidding me? Did you not just hear my cell phone speech? *(He realizes the ringing is coming from the backpack.)* Oh, wait, right—part of the play, forgot. Sorry. Never mind!

(The USHER *slinks off again as the young man pulls his head back in, horrified, looks toward his backpack about ten feet away, center, and begins a mad scramble to get to it—on his knees, rolling, crawling, whatever he has to do, he reaches for it, checking compartments, as the phone still rings, but he can't find it. Finally the phone stops ringing and of course just then—he finds it. He holds the phone up, looking at it as though he were disappointed in it. Just as he's about to turn off the ringer, it rings again and he reflexively answers it, hitting the ground low and whispering into it, his mouth close to the floor:)*

YOUNG MAN: Shuuuuush shush—whoever you are— please stop calling me. *(About to hang up, then)* Excuse me? Yes, this is he. I am in a most precarious

position right now and I can't--Yes, I will get back
to you at a more appropriate juncture—what do
you mean my Visa bill? You're calling me because
I'm behind on my—? Yes, I understand that I am in
arrears— "arrears" —yes, it is a word. Okay, I know
I am "behind" a month or two—okay, or eleven, and
I know as a credit card company—look, I'm in the
theatre, okay? We all have some ups and downs— Yes,
I am still gainfully employed—kind of. That is where
I am now in fact—that is why I am whispering—I am
backstage—Cats? No, we're not doing Cats. We're
doing A Christmas Carol— No, the play. We're doing
a theatrical dramatization of A Christmas Carol. No,
not with Jim Carrey. That was a movie. I'm about
fifteen feet from the stage—why does Visa care? Who
is playing Scrooge? Well, if you insist, it's Mr Hugh
Pendleton. Hugh Pendleton. Well, your never having
heard of him is not a reflection of his validity as a
practitioner of the art. I must say, I find you most rude
Mr Visa Card representative. Now as I said, I have to
go— the show is coming to an end, and I'm expected
to— yes, I shall pay it within the new year. Yes, I'm
aware of the deleterious effect it may have on my
credit rating— yes, it is a word. Goodbye Mr Visa Card
representative, and regardless of your tone, I wish you
a Merry Christmas.

(YOUNG MAN *hangs up. Finally turns off the ringer, then
hunches or crawls back toward the split in the curtain where
he catches up with the show. It's toward the end, where the
last strains of an acapella version of the* Wassail Song *plays,
then at a break in the song we hear the too sweet voice of
Tiny Tim from the stage—as the* YOUNG MAN *on his knees
sticks his head in, mouths the words along with the actor:)*

TINY TIM: "God Bless us all, everyone!"

(*The* YOUNG MAN *beams with pride. From the audience
[on the other side] we hear a detectable "sigh" with an*

*"Awww" or two thrown in as well, followed hard upon by
a smattering of applause. Suddenly, the distinct voice of a
grown* MAN:)

MAN: Ouuuuch!!!!!

(The YOUNG MAN *stops applauding. The* MAN *goes on:)*

MAN: Stop stabbing my foot you idiot! Get away from
me— oh for Cripes…

(As the applause suddenly dies down. The MAN's *voice
thunders once again from the other side of the drop:)*

MAN: MORON! How many times do I have to…

*(As we hear the actors on stage awkwardly start adlibbing,
trying to drown out the outburst, "Merry Christmas
everyone!" "Happy New Year!" etc. Suddenly, Hugh*
PENDLETON, *[the actor playing Scrooge], and dressed like
him, pushes through the split in the curtain, hobbling on one
foot. The* YOUNG MAN, *still on his knees, rolls out of the
way.)*

PENDLETON: Unbelievable! The crutch! She got me
again with her stupid crutch that doesn't even look
real!

(As the YOUNG MAN *on the floor, quickly gets up, rushes
to* PENDLETON, *who collapses in the chair in front of his
makeup mirror:)*

PENDLETON: Disaster!

YOUNG MAN: Are you okay, Mr Pendleton?

PENDLETON: Who the heck are you?

DEREK: Derek, props…

PENDLETON: Well, Erick Props…

DEREK: "Erick" is fine.

PENDLETON: Am I okay? Can you not see I've had a
major foot catastrophe? I've been stabbed!

(Suddenly, TINA *[as Tiny Tim] punches through the middle of the curtain behind* PENDLETON. *She is dressed as a typical Tim and "walking" on her knees, under which, are tied two Victorian era shoes in order to give the not very convincing illusion that she's a little boy. She is hobbling on a tiny white crutch as she makes a bee line for* PENDLETON. DEREK *tries to cut her off.)*

DEREK: Can I take your crutch, Tina?

TINA: *(Dead serious)* If you want to die.

*(*PENDLETON, *removing makeup, facing away from* TINA, *scowls:)*

PENDLETON: Don't go near that crutch! It's lethal. And about as convincing as her paper-thin characterization.

*(*TINA *raises the crutch, about to hit* PENDLETON *over the head with it when* DEREK *quickly intervenes, holding* TINA *back.* PENDLETON *has no idea.* TINA *quickly gains her composure, motions* DEREK *to let her go. He does, she takes a breath, turns toward* PENDLETON.*)*

TINA: What's the problem now, diva?

PENDLETON: If you stab my foot one more time with that phony looking midget crutch, I swear I'm gonna shove it up your...

*(*GEORGE *enters.)*

GEORGE: Hey, hey, hey—what happened out there?

PENDLETON: Only what is bound to happen when a professional is forced to work with a rank amateur.

TINA: Well maybe if you'd stop weaving all over the stage, I might know where I could put my friggin' crutch.

PENDLETON: Oh, I have an idea where you could put your friggin' crutch...

GEORGE: Alright, come on you two, lets both try to relax.

(TINA *remains on her knees, D L, removing her own makeup.*)

PENDLETON: Oh, would but I could, but I can't—because I have to share the stage with a female Tiny Tim— who can't act her way out of a paper bag!

TINA: Watch it old man!

(TINA *bangs the crutch on the floor, scaring* PENDLETON, *who reflexively lifts his foot.*)

GEORGE: Alright, Uncle Hugh, *(To* TINA*)* and my dearest wife—please—if you could both stop acting like seven-year-olds for one…

PENDLETON: I am doing the best I can to summon up a modicum of professionalism amid this tawdry, cut rate farce of a production.

GEORGE: This "farce" of a production, Uncle, pays for all the other plays you talk us into doing the rest of the season.

PENDLETON: Fine, but can you tell me—and with some amount of credibility, why Tiny Tim has a uterus exactly?

GEORGE: I made it clear at the read through: it adds an element of heightened, even magical realism.

PENDLETON: Oh, give it a rest Peter Brook. You don't even know what that means. You're just too cheap to hire a real actor.

TINA: Well excuse us. Sorry if we don't lavish more perks on you. We got you a stupid dresser, didn't we?

PENDLETON: What "dresser"?

(GEORGE *and* TINA *motion toward* DEREK, *who sweetly raises his hand.*)

PENDLETON: Who, Merrick? I thought he did props?

DEREK: Oh, I do those too— when I'm not in the box office or working front of house or concessions or...

PENDLETON: A fiasco, all of it!

TINA: And we'd have money left over if you didn't force us into doing that stupid Beckham play.

PENDLETON: It's "Beckett", not Beckham. He's an Irish dramatist, not an English soccer player.

TINA: Well, whatever his name is—that went over real well. "Waiting for Go Dot", or however you're supposed to pronounce it. And who ever heard of putting on a play where the guy in the title doesn't even show up? "Waiting for—SOMETHING TO HAPPEN" is what they should call that piece of crap.

PENDLETON: *(To* TINA*)* If you had even the slightest wafer-thin semblance of legitimate training, as some of us do—having attended...

GEORGE/PENDLETON/TINA: The Yale School of Drama.

PENDLETON: Indeed.

TINA: If he doesn't mention where he went to school at least once a day, his dentures pop out. Anyway, I'm outa here. *(To* GEORGE*)* Come on, we can't be late for our own cast party.

GEORGE: I'll meet you there. Just give me a sec.

TINA: Fine. *(To* PENDLETON*)* I'd wish you a Merry Christmas, but I wouldn't mean it.

PENDLETON: Thank you for sparing me the formality of having to concoct a civil reply.

TINA: Whatevs.

PENDLETON: And why are you still on your knees? Wait, don't tell me—it's how you got the part.

(TINA *just glares at him, then stands up, ripping the Tiny Tim shoes off her knees and tossing them at* DEREK, *who catches them.*)

TINA: Let's go.

DEREK: Yes, Tina.

(DEREK *follows* TINA *out.*)

(GEORGE *turns to* PENDLETON.)

GEORGE: You lied.

PENDLETON: Excuse me?

GEORGE: I know that isn't apple juice you've been drinking on stage. I can smell it on your breath. Everyone can.

PENDLETON: Are you accusing me…?

GEORGE: Look, uncle, you look down on us. You clearly think we, and this venue, are beneath you. But if you could just…

PENDLETON: I quit.

GEORGE: What?

PENDLETON: You heard me. I've had it. And you're right. This theatre *is* beneath me.

GEORGE: I'm sorry to hear you say that. We really have done everything we…

PENDLETON: Well, I wish I could say I was sorry but I'm not. I'll head back to civilization—to the city! Where talent like mine is appreciated.

GEORGE: I see. Well. I suppose you won't be joining us for the cast party.

PENDLETON: I humbly decline, thank you. But say "hey" to Tiny "Dim" for me. And do me a favor? Please don't cast her as Stanley in Streetcar next season, George. That really would be pushing it.

GEORGE: Goodnight, uncle.

PENDLETON: Goodnight.

(GEORGE *exits.* PENDLETON *waits a moment, then reaches into a small drawer in his makeup table and pulls out a flask, taking a swig.* DEREK *appears behind him.*)

DEREK: Is that a prop?

PENDLETON: *(Spooked)* What the…why are you sneaking up on me?

DEREK: It's my job to gather all the props before strike. That flask, is it a prop?

PENDLETON: Well, I suppose it is—in a manner of speaking. Who are you again?

DEREK: Derek. Your dresser, front of house, box office…

PENDLETON: Right.

(DEREK *starts to leave, then thinks better of it, steeling himself, then:*)

DEREK: I refuse to enable you Mr Pendleton.

PENDLETON: "Enable me" doing what?

DEREK: Drinking. Now if you'd be so kind, I'll have to ask you to check out of the theatre for the evening. I have to lock up and get home to Mr Marples before he starts to froth.

PENDLETON: "Mr Marples?"

DEREK: My cat.

PENDLETON: Your cat. I see. And he froths does he? At the mouth?

DEREK: Yes. And prodigiously. He's very old and I have to keep him in a carrier because his bones are brittle and he has seizures and, well…

PENDLETON: Sounds like a barrel of laughs, your cat.

DEREK: I don't require he be fun at this stage of his life—just comfortable.

PENDLETON: Right. You uh—you do a lot of things around here, but, let me guess—what you really want to do is act.

DEREK: *(Coy)* Maybe.

PENDLETON: Right, leave the keys with me, I'll lock up.

DEREK: I'm not sure that's okay.

PENDLETON: Don't worry. I promise I won't let anyone steal the forty seven year old sound system.

Derek hands him the keys.

DEREK: Please don't forget.

PENDLETON: *(Holding his up)* Pinky swear.

(DEREK starts out.)

PENDLETON: Oh, and one little piece of advice, before you go? From one old "broken down actor" to a new, hopeful one.

DEREK: Oh, thank you sir.

(PENDLETON gets out of his makeup chair, face to face with DEREK.)

PENDLETON: That little flame you have—inside—right here *(Touches DEREK's chest)*. The one that burns night and day—that keeps you hoping, aspiring, dreaming about being an actor. Do you know which one I'm talking about?

DEREK: Of course.

PENDLETON: Let it go out. *(As though extinguishing a candle flame with his fingers)* PFFFFFT. Just like that. Put it out yourself before the world does. Trust me, I just saved you forty years of regret and at least sixty grand worth of therapy. You can thank me later.

DEREK: Goodnight, Mr Pendleton.

PENDLETON: Goodnight, Hedwig.

DEREK: Derek.

PENDLETON: Right, got it.

(DEREK *leaves, dejected. As soon as he goes,* PENDLETON *walks over to a hidden bottle among the piles of old curtains or ropes and drinks from it, all the while mumbling "humbug" or "Mr Marples". He takes another healthy chug, then shuffles back to his makeup chair, where he begins to fall asleep. Gradually, we start to hear the sound of a single phone ringing from the stage area on the other side of the curtain. The* USHER *suddenly appears again.*)

USHER: *(To audience)* Seriously? With the phone again? Are you all messing with me? 'Cause I'm gonna lose it.

(It rings some more, USHER *suddenly realizes.)*

USHER: Oh, crap, wait. Sorry. Still part of the play. My bad.*(As he exits)* Guess I should have read the thing.

(Suddenly a spooky VOICE *is heard, resonating:)*

VOICE: Hugh Pendleton…

(PENDLETON jumps up, startled.)

PENDLETON: Wait, what? What was that?

(The single ringing phone continues as PENDLETON *gets up, reacting to it.)*

PENDLETON: A phone? Where the devil is that coming from?

(PENDLETON gets off the chair, starts to look around, under his makeup table, under the pile of ropes, etc. He notices the ringing coming from the other side of the backdrop.)

PENDLETON: In the theatre? What the—what is going on out there?

(*Suddenly we hear additional rings, all kinds of phones, antique, electronic, cell phones, beeping noises.* PENDLETON *starts toward the split in the curtain as the lights bump to black and now we hear a huge cocophony of ringing phones as a very quick change is made.*)

(*In the dark, the makeup table is converted to a working desk with an inkwell and feather pen on it, the pile of ropes and old curtains are removed to reveal a simple single bed and the backstage curtain is pulled down to reveal a simple and somewhat amateurly painted Dickensian street scene backdrop for "A Christmas Carol," a "Butcher Shop," "Boot Makers," etc., all paned windows with hints of snow. Also, two wooden side chairs, D R.*)

(*As the lights bump up, [hopefully in less than 10 seconds,] it appears* PENDLETON *never broke his stride and is now emerging through the middle of the curtain—walking directly onto the set of "A Christmas Carol" as the phone rings continue and he looks for their source, covering his ears:*)

PENDLETON: What is going on? What is this infernal ringing!?

(*Suddenly, appearing from the back of the house is a man dressed in a dated 70s style suit heavily strewn with old phones wrapped all around him—hanging from his waist, over his shoulders, everywhere. Old style cell phones, new phones, princess phones, desk phones, every kind of phone. Some even drag behind him. As the ringing continues,* PENDLETON *steps back, fearful. The man speaks:*)

APPARITION: Hughie, baby!

PENDLETON: Wait, what— Who are you? What is going on? And can you stop that clamorous ringing!?

(*The man/*APPARTITION *speaks to an unseen entity— skyward.*)

APPARITION: Hold my calls!

(The ringing suddenly stops.)

APPARITION: There, that's better, no?

PENDLETON: This is—this is ridiculous! Who—what the—what are you doing here? What is going on exactly?

APPARITION: Wait, you don't recognize me?

PENDLETON: Uhm, not really. Should I?

APPARITION: Well, we kinda fell out of touch. I was your agent.

PENDLETON: Wait, Marty? Marty Craver? Is that you?

MARTY: In the rotten flesh.

(One cell phone hanging off him starts to ring.)

MARTY: Oh, wait, sorry, I need to take this one.

PENDLETON: Fine, go ahead.

(MARTY takes the call, turning away from PENDLETON.)

MARTY: *(In phone)* Where are we at? Wait, what? Bullcrap! I told them forty over sixty and if they don't cave screw them to the wall! *(He hangs up)* Sorry, this deal I'm negotiating has no beginning, no middle, no end. I'm fated to be *this* close to closing, for eternity.

PENDLETON: Wait a minute— you don't even exist— why am I talking to you? You're an undigested speck of spicy tuna roll and nothing more.

MARTY: Don't be a fool, Hughie. I have much to tell and you would do well to…

(A phone rings again.)

MARTY: —ya know what, sorry, I really do have to take this one.

PENDLETON: Oh, for cripes sake.

MARTY: *(In phone)* Where we at? *(Pause)* We're going backwards call their bluff! *(He hangs up, looks to* PENDLETON*)* Sorry.

PENDLETON: Hey, Marty, what's with the uh—what's with the phone suit?

MARTY: These phones are but the chains that I did forge in life. I made them link by link, rolling the unused minutes into a dark chasm of eternity. And by the way, screw Verizon, seriously. They suck. You think you're screwed going over your minutes? Try calling from "eternity" —wait till you get that bill.

PENDLETON: I wouldn't know, I don't have Verizon. I'm actually not sure who I'm with— maybe it's uh…

MARTY: Hughie, you and I were very alike when we met those many years ago. I fed the beast of ambition inside you.

(Another of MARTY'*s phones ring.)*

MARTY: Don't worry, I'm ignoring it. Honestly I don't have to get it. *(Talking skyward)* I'm not a slave to this anymore. I mean sure, not answering is basically agent hell, but I could just…

PENDLETON: Oh, JUST ANSWER it!

MARTY: Thank you. *(He answers it. In phone:)* Talk to me! Well, will they give us a hard out? What? Screw them! *(He hangs up, then to* PENDLETON*)* The deal that never ends.

PENDLETON: Listen, Marty I feel bad, but—I didn't even know you died.

MARTY: Oh, no worries. There was a little mention of it in Variety. A very little mention actually. I don't think they would have written about it at all if it weren't for how I died.

PENDLETON: How did you die?

MARTY: Shark attack.

PENDLETON: You're kidding.

MARTY: I know, an agent eaten by a shark—a redundancy and an irony—all wrapped up in one.

PENDLETON: Why are you here exactly?

MARTY: I'm here to warn you Hugh Pendleton.

PENDLETON: About what?

MARTY: You have a chance, however slight, of escaping my fate.

PENDLETON: Oh, I'm not worried about that. I never go in the ocean.

MARTY: Not that fate, the after death one.

PENDLETON: Oh.

MARTY: This "second chance" is something I have negotiated for you as I feel a certain amount of guilt in your case.

PENDLETON: An agent feeling guilt? Now I know you don't exist.

MARTY: You once had a passion for your craft, a chance to be an actual artist.

PENDLETON: Oh, humbug—gotta stop saying that.

MARTY: You will be visited by three spirits.

PENDLETON: Three, seriously? That doesn't sound a little familiar to you at all?

MARTY: Expect the first tomorrow night, when the bell tolls one!

PENDLETON: They don't have Skype where you are?

MARTY: The second will appear on the next night at the same hour.

PENDLETON: Sorry, I'm planning on blacking out around then.

MARTY: And the third, on the following night.

PENDLETON: Ooops, sorry—that's my card night— solitaire, but still...

(MARTY *starts to move toward the back of the house, his voice echoes.)*

MARTY: Look upon me no more, Hugh Pendleton...

PENDLETON: Marty, cut it with the ghost voice, it's not scary.

MARTY: Okay, fine—I've exceeded my minutes anyway. But mark my words Hughie—mark my words. *(He starts moving toward the back of the house.)* And keep in touch, I mean that. We can do lunch at the Derby.

PENDLETON: What, the Brown Derby? That closed years ago.

MARTY: Not where I am. *(He points toward the floor)* Bwahahahahaaaaa!

(As MARTY *continues to laugh way too loudly, finally disappearing.* PENDLETON *looks around the set.)*

PENDLETON: Man, I gotta lay off the sauce. *(He goes to the bed on the set, reaches behind a pillow, pulls out a little bottle. Raises it to his mouth:)* And I will, as soon as I'm dead. *(He takes a healthy swig.)*

(Suddenly a bell tolls once.)

PENDLETON: Wait what? What the heck is that? I thought we couldn't afford bells?

(A VOICE *from the back of the house, echoing)*

VOICE: Shhhhhhhhhhhhhh!

(PENDLETON turns, looks out.)

PENDLETON: What?

VOICE: Shhhhuuush.

PENDLETON: What was that? Who just "shushed" me?

VOICE: Quiet please! Shhhhhhhhhhhhh...

PENDLETON: *(Looks around)* What the...?

(Emerging from back of the house is our USHER. *He's holding his flashlight, and not being shy about thrusting the bright beam right into people's eyes. He still has only one hand.)*

USHER: Voices down, please! *(He turns to some audience members, pointing his flashlight aggressively.)* And I should not have to say this again: purses out of the aisle and feet off the back of the chairs—puhleeez.

PENDLETON: Excuse me, who are you?

*(*USHER *points the light right into* PENDLETON's *eyes.)*

PENDLETON: *(Turns away from light)* Hey!

USHER: I sir, am the Usher of Christmas Past.

PENDLETON: The Usher of Christmas past? Crap, really—hey, wait, long past?

U C P: No, your past.

PENDLETON: I can't believe I walked into that.

U C P: Me either to be honest. *(He suddenly points his flashlight toward a back aisle.)* Did I just hear a candy wrapper? Who's crinkling? Do I have to give lessons on how to unwrap a piece of candy now? No "crinkly crinkly". Can we have a teensy weensy little bit of class for cripes sakes?

PENDLETON: Wow, you are one angry usher.

U C P: We're all angry, buddy. Angry ushers are theatre's deep dark little secret.

PENDLETON: And you're here to do what exactly?

U C P: "Usher" you—back in time. Get it? See what I did there? *(He suddenly points the flashlight toward the audience, in someone's face.)* Are you texting? Turn it off! Yup, you! I am watching you D7. *(Does fingers to eyes threat.)* Oh, I'm on you. I am on you. *(Suddenly points to another audience member.)* You find that funny G4? Huh? Because I don't, and I'm watching you too. *(Back to PENDLETON)* What the heck happened to decorum at the theatre? Seriously. When I started in this job, men and women *dressed* for the theatre. That's right, people dressed! *(Pointing to someone in back)* And by dressed, I don't mean sweatpants and tuxedo tee shirts. That's right, and no talking either. You're not in your living room watching "The Voice." There are real human beings up here, okay? They can *hear* you. So don't talk to them. Just watch it, all of you, because I have seriously had it! *(To PENDLETON)* You— *(Pointing)* four down and three in please.

PENDLETON: What?

U C P: You heard me, I'm directing you to your seat. It's what we do. Walk fours rows down, slide three seats in please.

PENDLETON: You want me to sit in the audience?

U C P: Four down, three over and take my hand!

PENDLETON: Your hand? What are you talking about?

U C P: Oh, forget it. *(He walks back to the seat in question, shines his light right in the audience member's face.)* You, C6—right, sorry to wake ya. Do me a solid and reach under your seat please?

(The patron [hopefully] does.)

U C P: Come on, give a guy a hand, will ya?

(The patron by now has hopefully pulled out a disturbingly real looking hand, some fake blood, tendons still attached, with a little bone sticking out.)

U C P: Great, toss it here.

(The patron tosses the hand to U C P.*)*

U C P: Perfect. *(Walks back to* PENDLETON*)* Pendleton, take my hand.

*(*U C P *tosses it toward* PENDLETON, *who runs away from it. It thumps on the floor.)*

PENDLETON: Ewwwwwwww! Iccccck! Cripes, that is— yuk, that is gross! How did you—how did you lose it?

U C P: Ferris wheel accident.

PENDLETON: Ewww— cripes, is that how you died?

U C P: No. I was killed by a shark, actually.

PENDLETON: You're kidding?

U C P: Why would I kid about something like that?

PENDLETON: What is it with all these shark deaths? Is this some kind of weird rule, where all my spirits have to be killed by sharks?

U C P: Why can't it just be a coincidence?

PENDLETON: Were you swimming or…

U C P: I was at a restaurant.

PENDLETON: A shark got you at a restaurant? Was it right on the water, or…

U C P: No, I ate some sushi. Mako shark. It was tainted. I developed a bacterial infection, and within thirty-two minutes was dead as a doornail.

PENDLETON: Holy cripes, that is horrible.

U C P: I wasn't fun, no. *(He offers the hand to* PENDLETON.*)* Take my hand, Pendleton!

PENDLETON: What? Are you kidding? I'm not touching that thing, it's gross.

U C P: Take it!

PENDLETON: Fine!

(PENDLETON *touches the hand, and suddenly a thunder crack—and sounds of loud wind—as by now he has grabbed onto it and the hand starts leading him around the stage in a large circle, the lights flickering, thunder and wind blowing as* U C P *stays in once place, remotely guiding* PENDLETON *around the stage by pointing his handless arm in his direction until finally,* PENDLETON *comes to a stop and the lights shift, suddenly denoting a green pastoral setting, the storm sounds recede and we hear the gentle sounds of birds in the background.* PENDLETON *looks around, getting his bearings.)*

PENDLETON: Wait, is this—could it be?

U C P: It could.

(U C P *takes his hand back.)*

PENDLETON: Penner's Lake Day Camp. I spent summers here as a boy.

(*We hear the sound of kids playing in the distance.* PENDLETON *looks across the field, sees something.)*

PENDLETON: Hey, isn't that Hankins over there? My old counselor?

U C P: It is.

PENDLETON: (*Looking all over*) And the boathouse, cabins, the little beach. It's like I'm back.

U C P: You are back. Back where it all began.

PENDLETON: Where what began?

(*Off, we hear the sound of kids bullying, yelling, making fun of someone.* PENDLETON *looks toward the sounds.)*

PENDLETON: Hey, what are those kids doing? Are they ganging up on that little boy? Where did Hankins go? (*Calling out*) Hey, Hankins!?

U C P: Hankins is rolling a fat one in the boat house.

PENDLETON: Well, tell those bullies to lay off that little kid!

U C P: You don't recognize that "little kid"?

PENDLETON: *(Shouting, again)* Hey, leave him alone!

U C P: They can't hear you. Another dimension, remember?

(Suddenly, a somewhat cool looking boy [JEFFREY] appears, screaming toward the bullies.)

JEFFREY: Hey! Ball-less wonders!

(The sound of bullying stops.)

JEFFREY: I thought that would get your attention.

PENDLETON: *(Recognizing)* Hey, is that?

U C P: It most certainly is.

PENDLETON: Jeffrey? Jeffrey Hoberman.

U C P: The one and only.

(JEFFREY keeps yelling toward the unseen bullies.)

JEFFREY: Hey, where ya goin' lunk heads? What, scared to pick on somebody your own size? Wait, I'm sorry, did I just use too many syllables?

(PENDLETON steps forward.)

PENDLETON: Jeff, it's me, Hugh!

U C P: He can't see you.

PENDLETON: Oh, is there anything you can do?

U C P: Alright, back off.

(U C P reaches into a small side pocket, then throws some invisible substance straight into PENDLETON's eyes. Sound of pixie dust?)

PENDLETON: Ouch, well for cripes sake, what was that?

U C P: Magical "whatever" dust. Note to self—throw below eyes.

(JEFFREY *turns right to* PENDLETON.)

JEFFREY: You okay, kid? They didn't rough you up, did they?

PENDLETON: He sees me.

U C P: As you used to be, not as you are. That was the dust thing.

JEFFREY: Don't let those Neanderthals treat you like that. Just use big words on them, like "cat" or "door". It'll throw 'em off every time.

PENDLETON: Thank you for saving me.

JEFFREY: Forget about it. Hey, come by the theatre after chow.

PENDLETON: Me?

JEFFREY: No, the guy standing next to you.

PENDLETON: You see him?

JEFFREY: Who?

U C P: (*To* PENDLETON) Weird coincidence.

JEFFREY: You ever act before?

PENDLETON: Like in a theatre?

JEFFREY: No, like in a muffler shop, yes in a theatre. Come and audition tonight. You'll fit right in.

PENDLETON: Really?

JEFFREY: Well, you clearly don't fit anywhere else. See ya tonight buddy.

PENDLETON: Wait, Jeffrey…

(JEFFREY *exits.*)

U C P: He's gone.

PENDLETON: He was the nicest person. He became a brilliant composer you know, Broadway, off-Broadway, he could do it all.

U C P: And died too young.

PENDLETON: So many did. Hey, that was the moment, wasn't it, when I first thought about being...

(U C P offers his "hand" again.)

U C P: Take my hand, Pendleton, we've got a schedule to keep.

PENDLETON: Oh, no, no thanks. Are you telling me there's no other way you can jettison me through time other than touching a gross decapitated hand? Honestly, it's not very appealing.

U C P: I don't care! Take my hand!

(PENDLETON reluctantly takes it, thunder clap again—as the hand whisks him off running again, as U C P stays where he is, guiding him from where he stands. Wind noise, flashing lights, etc., as they travel in a quick circle and PENDLETON comes back toward the single bed—on which is sitting a lovely, pregnant young woman. PENDLETON sees her, beside himself:)

PENDLETON: Kate? Kate! *(Turns to U C P)* That's my sister Kate!

U C P: It is indeed.

PENDLETON: So beautiful.

U C P: Her first year as a teacher.

PENDLETON: *(Trying to get her attention)* Hey, Kate! Kate, it's me! Hugh! Kate...

U C P: She can't hear you. What are you not getting about the convention I set up?

PENDLETON: Well, throw some of that stuff at me! Hit me!

U C P: Are you sure? Sometimes going back makes it harder.

PENDLETON: Just get me back there!

(U C P *throws some invisible dust in his face.* PENDLETON *turns to his sister and she immediately stands, goes to hug him.*)

KATE: Baby brother!

PENDLETON: Oh, Kate. *(He turns to* U C P.*)* Wait, this is when I told her…

(U C P *hands* PENDLETON *a legal sized envelope.*)

U C P: You asked for it.

(PENDLETON *turns back to her, holding up the envelope, suddenly forlorn.*)

PENDLETON: Got this today.

KATE: You finally heard?

PENDLETON: Uh, yeah. Afraid so.

KATE: Oh, Hugh, listen, if it's not the news you wanted to hear you can't despair. You are such a brilliant actor and there are only a million other schools you can apply to. What did they say? *(She grabs the envelope out of his hand, opens it. Starts to read)*

PENDLETON: Just a stupid form letter.

KATE: *(Reading)* "Dear Mr Pendleton, we are very pleased to inform you…" *(Realizes, looks over at him)* You rotten bugger! *(Hugs him immediately)* You got in! You did it, Hugh, I'm so proud!

PENDLETON: Don't get too excited, I still have to find a way to pay for it.

KATE: I still have some money mommy left me. I know you blew through yours.

PENDLETON: Don't be silly, you're going to need it.

KATE: Oh, shut up, let me help my baby brother. Think of how proud they'd be, Hugh. I'll come up to New Haven in the fall and make sure you're not starving to death.

(PENDLETON *turns to* U C P.)

PENDLETON: I'd like to go back now.

U C P: There's more.

KATE: I'm so proud of you. You're getting out of this stupid little town. I'm so glad one of us will.

U C P: She never made it to New Haven, did she? She died soon after your nephew was born, the same nephew you...

PENDLETON: Alright, that's enough.

U C P: She believed in you, when no one else did.

PENDLETON: I said enough!

U C P: Fine, then have a seat.

PENDLETON: Have a seat where?

(U C P *grabs the two wooden chairs and places them D C, facing away from the audience. He shines his flashlight in* PENDLETON's *face, then shines it on one of the seats.)*

U C P: Here!

PENDLETON: But what if I don't wanna...

(A thunderclap, as U C P *shines the light on the chair again.)*

U C P: I said sit!

PENDLETON: Fine!

(The lights shift on the chairs, and it seems like a new theatre entirely as PENDLETON *looks around, amazed.)*

PENDLETON: Whoa, wait—is this where I think it is?

U C P: It is.

PENDLETON: Adams Memorial Theatre.

PENDLETON and U C P both sit on the chairs, facing the set of "A Christmas Carol.")

U C P: Where you made your professional debut.
Summer stock.

*(A rumpled, middle-aged man [BIRDY] walks out onto the
stage, looks out toward the audience:)*

BIRDY: Is anyone still here? Have we chased you all
away?

PENDLETON: Birdy! That's Birdy!

U C P: Thaddeus T Byrd, artistic director. Founded The
Berkshire Summer Theatre on the back of a flat bed
truck. Ran it for almost forty years.

PENDLETON: Amazing fellow, brilliant imagination.
He's about to give his end of summer talk.

BIRDY: Are you all broke? Exhausted? Do you feel
completely taken advantage of? Good—then you've
had a good summer.

PENDLETON: He said the same thing every year, but I
didn't care. Every time he said it, it sounded new.

U C P: Truth has no expiration date.

BIRDY: First thing I want you all to do, is forget
everything you think you learned here. I want you to
be a beginner every single day of your artistic life.

PENDLETON: He could have directed on Broadway.

U C P: He never had that kind of ambition.

PENDLETON: He died broke ya know. Lived in that
same crappy little walk up above Pappa Charlie's Deli
his whole life.

U C P: Funny, I always considered him having died
rich, just not with money.

BIRDY: If I could convince you of anything, each
and every one of you, it would be to never forget
this moment. This one, right now. *(Suddenly looking
toward PENDLETON)* Scared what's next for you? Good,

be scared. *(Back to others)* If you find yourself too comfortable anywhere, leave immediately. But know this: it will never be this beautiful, this innocent—this magical, again.

PENDLETON: He was right.

U C P: Yes, he was.

BIRDY: The world is going to do its best to take the breath out of you. Don't let it. And don't forget us back here. *(Again, to* PENDLETON*)* You'll always have a home. *(Back to others)* Now go! And don't hug one another so much, it's unbecoming. No tears! Learn how to leave people. If you're lucky you'll be doing it over and over again, now go! Fly! *(Exits)*

PENDLETON: "Learn how to leave people."

(U C P points across the stage. The lights change to reflect trees, greenery. Standing there is a beautiful young woman, SUSAN. PENDLETON *turns, sees her.)*

PENDLETON: Is that?

U C P: It is.

(U C P sprinkles a little dust behind his head. SUSAN *turns, faces him.)*

SUSAN: There's nothing to apologize for, Hugh. Of course you should go.

*(*PENDLETON *gets out of the chair, walks into the scene with* SUSAN.*)*

PENDLETON: But you're disappointed, Susan, just admit it.

SUSAN: I'm disappointed we won't have our season together, of course. It was what we always wanted. Or what you said, anyway. They offered us an entire season. They offered us brilliant roles. That isn't a usual thing.

PENDLETON: Well we are amazing together. But Minneapolis?

SUSAN: A beautiful town that appreciates theatre. Is there a problem with that, Hugh?

PENDLETON: Well, in terms of who might actually see us, yes. What industry is there up there, what's the market like?

SUSAN: "Industry"? "Market"?

PENDLETON: Look, just because I want to be seen by a lot of people doesn't mean I'm a sell out, okay?

SUSAN: I didn't say you were.

PENDLETON: My agent said I have to commit to LA now or never, that there's a window.

SUSAN: Windows open and close all the time, Hugh. That's the nature of windows.

PENDLETON: I'll fly back every couple of weeks.

SUSAN: Actually, there's no need.

PENDLETON: What? What does that mean?

SUSAN: I think we should rethink things.

PENDLETON: Like what?

SUSAN: We're on different paths. I want to act. You want to be famous. Lately all you talk about is business, markets, deals. We used to talk about plays, ideas. We used to talk about art.

PENDLETON: So your dream is worthy, mine isn't. Is that it?

SUSAN: No, yours is worthy, it just isn't mine. I wish you all the happiness I really do.

(SUSAN *kisses* PENDLETON *on the cheek. He turns to* U C P.)

PENDLETON: Spare me this will you? Get this stupid dust out of my eyes and get me out of here.

SUSAN: Goodbye, Hugh.

(PENDLETON *can't bear to turn around and look at* SUSAN *again. She withdraws. He looks at* U C P.)

PENDLETON: You find this entertaining, do you?

U C P: We have one more shadow to pass through.

PENDLETON: No more shadows!

(U C P *waves his arm and there's a thunder clap. Suddenly, appearing in a pool of light on the other side of the stage is* MARTY, PENDLETON's *agent, only younger. He speaks into a phone.*)

MARTY: No, no, no, I get it, believe me. He doesn't ring your bell. Look, he came out here to the West coast a couple years ago and he had a little heat but things change. Hugh Pendleton is nowhere now. Besides, I just signed somebody a whole lot fresher, a whole lot newer and with a lot more heat.

(PENDLETON *turns to* U C P.)

PENDLETON: I don't want to see anymore.

U C P: Hey, don't blame the usher if you don't like the show.

PENDLETON: I said, get me out of here!

U C P: Fine, be that way. (*Toward the audience, pointing his flashlight in several faces*) As for all of you, it's intermission. You've got fifteen minutes to get your butts back here. And by the way, would it kill you to buy some watered down wine and stale cookies while you're out there? (*He should pitch whatever else the theatre is selling. Back to* PENDLETON) And as for you Hugh Pendleton, good luck! You're gonna need it!

(U C P's laughter echoes loudly as he disappears, and the lights fade to black as music comes up.)

END OF ACT ONE

ACT TWO

(*As the music fades and lights come up, we see Pendleton sleeping in the bed on the set. Suddenly, a bell tolls.* PENDLETON *wakes up in a start, reflexively counting "one" on his hand, as he jumps out of bed.*)

PENDLETON: Okay, that was one.

(*We hear another toll.* PENDLETON *counts "two" on his hand.*)

PENDLETON: Two rings. Oh, crap. I'm gonna need a little sustenance.

(PENDLETON *turns back to the bed, sits at the foot of it, and reaches under a cover for another hidden bottle. Just as he's about to drink from it we hear a booming female* VOICE *over the God Mic.*)

VOICE: Hold please.

(PENDLETON *looks back toward the booth, confused.*)

PENDLETON: Wait, what? Hold what? Who is that?

VOICE: I said just stay still please, we're setting.

PENDLETON: What do you mean "setting"? What is going on!?

VOICE: Alright, everybody, I'm calling a five. Clearly we're having a little "actor problem".

(*Suddenly appearing from the back of the house is a* WOMAN *dressed casually with a pony tail, a backwards facing baseball cap, a tool belt with various rolls of tape hanging off it and a stop watch around her neck.)*

WOMAN: Would you get off the bed please?

PENDLETON: What? Why?

WOMAN: We have to move it downstage, that's why, now get off it. Come on, off, off, off, off, off.

(PENDLETON hops off.)

PENDLETON: Alright, fine, but this is highly peculiar.

WOMAN: Yeah, whatever buddy. Clear please.

(WOMAN pushes PENDLETON aside, then gets on her knees, moving the bed a couple inches. She looks up toward the booth for an okay.)

WOMAN: Here? No? Crap. *(She moves it back.)* Back there? No? *(Looks at PENDLETON)* Will you get out of my light please? I'm trying to be very precise here.

PENDLETON: Fine.

WOMAN: *(Moves it again)* Okay, what about down here? Good? *(Gets the okay)* Good!

PENDLETON: What's the point exactly? The show is closed.

WOMAN: Oh, my shows never close buddy. My shows never close.

PENDLETON: And who are you?

WOMAN: Stage Manager of Christmas Present, that's who.

PENDLETON: You've got to be kidding me.

S M C P: I'm a stage manager, buddy—I don't have a sense of humor. Downstage two feet please?

PENDLETON: What?

S M C P: You heard me, move down!

PENDLETON: Why!?

S M C P: Because you're out of the light, that's why.
Now move!

(PENDLETON *moves down a couple feet.*)

S M C P: Good, thank you. Now, grab my tape.

(S M C P *turns and sticks her hip out, offering* PENDLETON
a couple rolls of tape to pick from.)

PENDLETON: What do you mean "grab your tape"?
Why would I do that?

S M C P: Because I said, that's why. Now grab hold of
my tape or we're not going anywhere.

PENDLETON: But it's just weird, I don't even know you,
and you want me to…

S M C P: Grab it!

(*Just as* PENDLETON *grabs a roll of tape, thunder cracks,
as* S M C P *leads him around the stage, through the
"air", holding her arm up as though she was flying like a
superhero. The sound of wind, flickering lights. Finally, they
land around center, as the light changes. We hear the sound
of street traffic.*)

PENDLETON: What is this place? Where are we?

S M C P: Just outside of town, on the "other side of the
tracks". Not a Starbucks or Old Navy in sight.

PENDLETON: (*Looking*) 10 Woodland Road? This place
looks like a flop house.

S M C P: Not to the people who live in it. Inside this
"flop house" —a dream is dying.

PENDLETON: What does this have to do with me?

(S M C P *offers the tape on her hip again.*)

S M C P: Hold my tape, we're going inside.

PENDLETON: What? No, I'm not touching your tape anymore. It makes me uncomfortable.

S M C P: Ya wanna be Equity deputy for eternity?

(PENDLETON *grabs the tape.*)

PENDLETON: Let's go.

(*Wind and noise as lights flash and* PENDLETON *and* S M C P *"fly" [meaning run in one small circle], basically "landing" exactly where they started. He has a look around, covering his nose.*)

PENDLETON: Ughhh—what is that smell?

S M C P: I've been dead a while, so it might be me. But more likely it's cat urine.

PENDLETON: "Cat urine?" By the way, how did you die?

S M C P: Wow, that's kind of personal.

PENDLETON: You weren't killed by a shark, were you?

S M C P: How did you know that?

PENDLETON: What the heck is it with sharks?

S M C P: Oh, I wasn't killed by a "shark" shark. I fell down the stairs, broke my neck in seven places and lingered there at the bottom for four days before my heart finally gave out. I wasn't a very "social" person. Seems that kind of makes a difference when you find yourself slowly dying at the bottom of the stairs—for days on end.

PENDLETON: Wow, that's—that's horrible.

S M C P: It wasn't a barrel of monkeys.

PENDLETON: But what does it have to do with a shark?

S M C P: That's what I tripped on.

PENDLETON: There was a shark at the top of your stairs?

S M C P: Yeah, they're little vacuum cleaners. You never heard of them?

PENDLETON: I haven't.

S M C P: Well here's a little hint, free of charge. Don't leave 'em at the top of your stairs.

PENDLETON: Duly noted. (*Looks around*) Cripes what kind of dump is this?

S M C P: The only kind he can afford.

PENDLETON: Who?

(DEREK *enters, carrying a small portable cat carrier, a can of something and a Dixie cup.*)

DEREK: Okay, Mr Marples! Daddy hasn't forgotten you.

PENDLETON: Oh, the kid from the theatre. That's right, he's got a cat.

S M C P: Mr Marples. The one you made fun of.

PENDLETON: Well come on, a cat? Really?

(DEREK *places the carrier on one of the chairs, sits on the other chair in front of it.*)

DEREK: Alright, Mr "M" —no more grumbly in that tumbly, it is yum yum time! Wanna start with some milk? (*He offers Mr Marples inside the carrier some milk. Mr Marples doesn't take to it.*) Please, Mr M, just try a little harder.

S M C P: Mr Marples is all he as left. His mother died three years ago, his father ten years before that. That cat is his entire world. And you belittled it.

PENDLETON: Oh, come on. (He moves closer, peeks toward the inside of the carrier, recoils.) Ewwww, yikes! Wow, that is one mangy looking cat! And he wasn't kidding, it does froth at the mouth.

S M C P: It's more than twenty years old, give it a break! Poor thing can barely walk.

DEREK: *(To Mr Marples)* Alright, then, if milk is not to your liking, I am happy to say we have a very special entree for you this fine Christmas Eve—and you're gonna eat it all up. *(He produces the small can of tuna.)* Voila! That's right, *(In French accent)* Chicken of the Sea! And it's all yours! *(He peels back the lid, slides the can into the carrier, watching. Clearly disappointed)* Oh, please eat, Mr. Marples. You have to keep up your strength. Just a little. Please? *(Mr Marples doesn't eat.)*

PENDLETON: Holy crud this is depressing. So, is the foaming little dust bag gonna make it or not?

S M C P: *(Looking off)* I see an empty carrier placed near the trash heap in front of this dilapidated building. I see a young man giving up on his dream, but then that's what you told him to do isn't it? "Pfffft. Let the flame go out."

PENDLETON: Oh, come on.

(DEREK raises the little Dixie cup of milk.)

DEREK: A toast, Mr Marples. To Hugh Pendleton!

(We hear Mr Marples hiss loudly from inside the kennel.)

DEREK: Oh, now be nice Mr Marples. Yes, he's a grumpy ol' sourpuss and a bitter old fart...

PENDLETON: Hey!

DEREK: ...and yes, he did say some devastatingly mean, toxic and destructive things to me tonight, but we must remember that at one time, believe it or not, he was a most brilliant actor. He inspired me.

PENDLETON: Hey, I inspired him.

S M C P: Oh, shut up.

(DEREK toasts.)

DEREK: To Hugh Pendleton! A long life and a Merry Christmas!

(We hear a resigned little "meow" from the kennel.)

DEREK: Oh, Mr Marples you are most adorable!

(DEREK collects the carrier and exits. S M C P turns to PENDLETON.)

S M C P: Alright, you just stay where you are. I gotta go scrub this cat piss smell off me. I think I got some Ajax in the booth. *(She starts walking toward the back of house.)*

PENDLETON: Wait, what are you gonna do, just leave me here? Aren't I between worlds or in purgatory or something? What if I can't get back? What if…

S M C P: Oh, for cripes sake, Pendleton. You're an actor, aren't ya? Act like you have a pair. I'll be watching. Trust me, I'm always watching!

(S M C P laughs as she exits. Just as she does, GEORGE appears behind PENDLETON, raising a glass to a room of unseen guests, as we hear the sound of a party, under.)

GEORGE: To my always amazing cast and crew: I want to thank you all for a wonderful, albeit, somewhat rocky season. I thank you for your dedication, for your hard work and most of all for your patience—especially tonight.

(PENDLETON steps up, looks toward the booth, addressing an unseen S M C P.)

PENDLETON: It's the stupid cast party, I said I didn't want to go!

GEORGE: I know my uncle can often be a…challenge? But strange as it may seem for me to feel this way, part of me wishes he had shown up tonight.

(TINA enters with a drink.)

TINA: Are you insane? That ingrate took a crap on everything we stand for.

GEORGE: Still, dearest, he is my uncle and at one point was a pretty amazing man.

TINA: Yeah, decades ago.

GEORGE: There was a time when people regarded him highly, with real esteem even.

TINA: Yeah, *(Pick current public pariah)* Bill Cosby too—how did that work out?

PENDLETON: Hey, low blow.

GEORGE: *(To* TINA*)* But who does he hurt, when he acts like he does, except himself? He seems determined to be mean to us, but who ends up alone? Him. I'm sorry, but I refuse to give up on my mother's brother. *(Raising his glass)* To Hugh Pendleton!

TINA: You can't be serious.

GEORGE: As serious as my boundless love for you, my dear wife.

(We hear "awww" from the unseen guests. TINA *raises her glass, reluctantly.)*

TINA: Alright, to the old goat. I guess.

(Lights down on GEORGE *and* TINA, *highlighting* PENDLETON, *who watches them go.)*

PENDLETON: My goodness…they still raise a glass in my honor.

(We hear S M C P's *booming voice over the mic.)*

S M C P: Alright, next scene! Three steps upstage Pendleton, now!

PENDLETON: Wait, what? Why do I have to move upstage?

S M C P: Because I said. Do you want to go back to cat piss house?

PENDLETON: Alright, fine—three steps. *(He moves three steps upstage.)*

S M C P: Wow, look who learned to take direction.

PENDLETON: Alright, now what?

S M C P: Two steps left.

PENDLETON: Fine. *(He takes two steps left, finds himself in front of the foot of the bed.)* Now what?

S M C P: Plant it!

(PENDLETON quickly sits on the end of the bed.)

PENDLETON: There. Now what? Cripes, this is like *No Exit*, except hell isn't "other people," it's other theatre people.

(A bell tolls. PENDLETON looks concerned.)

PENDLETON: Ugh, here we go again.

(It tolls again.)

PENDLETON: Aaaaaand… *(It tolls a third time)* There, bingo, number three. Ominous bell tolls: never a good thing.

(Suddenly a MAN walks from the audience area, right onto the stage. He's dressed in a conservative sport coat, with elbow patches. He's wearing glasses and carrying a notebook and a pen. PENDLETON just looks at him. The man ignores PENDLETON for the most part, just walks around the stage a little, jotting a couple notes down in his book. PENDLETON tries to get his attention:)

PENDLETON: Uhm—excuse me?

(The MAN ignores him. Continues to examine the set, clearly not impressed, even scoffing a little.)

PENDLETON: Yeah, uhm— hi? I'm just curious, if you don't mind, who are you exactly?

(The MAN *sits right next to* PENDLETON *on the end of the bed, writing intensely into his notebook. He continues to ignore* PENDLETON *as* PENDLETON *just watches him.* PENDLETON *gets up, turning to him:)*

PENDLETON: Okay, you're either an incredibly rude audience member with no sense whatsoever of the fourth wall, or you're my third spirit. Which is it?

(The MAN *takes off his glasses, smiles at* PENDLETON, *smugly, holding up three fingers.)*

PENDLETON: Crap, I knew it.

(The MAN *smiles.)*

PENDLETON: Ugh. Third spirits are always the worst.

*(*PENDLETON *sits beside* MAN *again, as the* MAN *continues to jot things down in his notebook.)*

PENDLETON: Look buddy, this ain't my first rodeo. Okay? I get it. I was a jerk. I shouldn't be. You all haunt me, I learn some stuff and I stop being a jerk, okay, fine, now go home. Show's over.

*(*MAN *ignores* PENDLETON.*)*

PENDLETON: Listen, seriously: I am not going to cooperate with you in any way whatsoever until you answer two questions: 1), who are you? And 2), were you killed by a shark?

(The MAN *holds up the notebook.)*

PENDLETON: A notebook. Oh-kay.

(The MAN *holds up the pen in his other hand.)*

PENDLETON: And…a pen. Right.

(The MAN *then puts pen to paper, writes something in the notebook. Shows it to* PENDLETON, *who reads it.)*

PENDLETON: "The Critic of Christmas Yet to Come." Oh, crap, really?

(C C Y C *nods yes.* PENDLETON *gets up again.*)

PENDLETON: And don't tell me: like any third spirit worth his salt, you don't talk, do you?

(C C Y C *smiles, nods no.*)

PENDLETON: Right. You write.

(C C Y C *nods yes, holding up pen.*)

PENDLETON: Gotchya. But do tell me, oh "illustrious critic". You are here to critique my life, are you not? To "review" me—as you show me things that are yet to pass?

(C C Y C *slowly raises his arm, pointing behind* PENDLETON.)

PENDLETON: Oh, no no no—we're not doing that silent pointy thing with the arm, —that's very "third spirit" of you, but I'm not falling for that anymore. Lest you forget buddy, I've played this part a thousand times, just never as myself. I know I'm supposed to say "I don't care what the critics say", or that "I don't read reviews", but every actor who says that is full of crap, lets face it. I mean I don't read reviews—I have my friends read them to me.

(C C Y C *points. Loud thunder crack.*)

PENDLETON: Alright! Fine—fine! I've done this more than you have buddy.

(PENDLETON *looks over to where* C C Y C *is pointing as suddenly a light comes up, illuminating two hipster actors at a coffee shop in L A, [one female], both reading off their phones.*)

ACTOR 1: (*Female*) Oh hey, look who died. (*Shows phone*)

ACTOR 2: Oh yeah, I kinda remember him.

PENDLETON: "Kinda?"

ACTOR 2: He was in *Spaceballs*, wasn't he?

PENDLETON: *Spaceballs!? (Toward actor)* Hey wise aleck, for your information, I passed on Spaceballs!

(The ACTORS *disappear.* PENDLETON *continues his rant.)*

PENDLETON: *Spaceballs?* Seriously? Like I'm not above that kind of drek. And besides, they wouldn't meet my quote. *(To* C C Y C*)* There is no way they are talking about me—no way!

(C C Y C *points once again toward the other side of the stage. Lights up as* PENDLETON *looks over there.)*

PENDLETON: Holy crap, what kind of dumpy room is that?

*(Two figures [*LOW LIFES*] emerge, one male, one female, both shady characters. They are bent over a cardboard box with the initials "H P" on it. One holds up a little plaque.)*

LOW LIFE 1: *(Female)* An Ovation Award?" What the heck is this?

LOW LIFE 2: I have no idea, and I don't care. He was some kind of actor, wasn't he?

LOW LIFE 1: So he said. Look, I just delivered the old guy's medicine. He was a really bitter old dude.

LOW LIFE 2: See if there's a real award in there, one that matters, not these stupid plaques. Maybe there's an Oscar or something.

LOW LIFE 1: Are you kidding? If he had an Oscar, do you think he'd live in this crap hole?

PENDLETON: Hey, have a little respect!

(LOW LIFE 2 pulls another plaque out.)

LOW LIFE 2: Hey, here's something.

LOW LIFE 1: What?

LOW LIFE 2: *(Reads inscription)* "Best Actor, Secaucus Film Festival, Secaucus, New Jersey."

LOW LIFE 1: Wow, big time.

*(*LOW LIFES *both laugh loudly as they disappear.*
PENDLETON *sits stunned.)*

PENDLETON: Alright, enough! Is there no one that cared for that wretched fellow?

(Lights shift as DEREK *comes back on stage carrying his little cat carrier. He places it on one of the chairs, sits across from it.)*

DEREK: Mr Marples, you will never believe what I did today. I took the crosstown bus all the way to Hillside Cemetery to visit his final resting place. It's not terribly kept up I'm afraid, and there's still no marker, though I know George is doing his best to raise funds for that very purpose. But ever since his theatre closed, I think he's been having challenges of his own to tell you the truth.

PENDLETON: *(To* C C Y C*)* "Closed?" George's theatre closed?

*(*C C Y C *smiles a little, pleased, then points back to* DEREK.*)*

DEREK: I put a copy of *King Lear* on his grave. So at least there's something.

*(*PENDLETON *turns to* C C Y C.*)*

PENDLETON: You should have seen me in that. I killed it.

*(*C C Y C *rolls his eyes, turns away from* PENDLETON, *makes the gagging gesture with his finger down his throat.* DEREK *stands, still addressing the carrier.)*

DEREK: Oh, Mr Marples I should stop this, I know. This isn't healthy. A psychiatrist would have a field day, but it helps. It does. Talking to you like this. Or, pretending to anyway. I miss you so much, my friend. *(He moves to the kennel, opens the front and slowly pulls out Mr Marple's small red collar. There's a tiny bell on it, that rings a little when he holds it.)* You were so light to carry, and no trouble at all. *(He exits with carrier.)*

PENDLETON: Oh well, I am sorry about that. Poor creature. I suppose in its own mangy, frothing at the mouth way, it wasn't an entirely disagreeable cat.

(C C Y C glares toward PENDLETON, *then gets up, closing his notebook, walking away.* PENDLETON *follows him.)*

PENDLETON: But hold on, hold on—what that kid said there, he said with such certainty. As though it's already come to pass, but that's not true, is it spirit?

(C C Y C looks at PENDLETON *with disgust and pity, shaking his head. He then turns to leave again, as* PENDLETON *urgently follows him.)*

PENDLETON: No, wait, stop!

(C C Y C stops.)

PENDLETON: Look, this is a question I've asked as Scrooge a thousand times before, but it's the only time I've actually cared what the answer is. Tell me, are these the shadows of things that might be or the shadow of things that will be?

(An ominous bell tolls as a pin spot suddenly illuminates something resting on top of the bed, glowing under the light. PENDLETON *sees it.)*

PENDLETON: What is that? A newspaper? Well, that's different. Since when does Scrooge see a newspaper?

(C C Y C points toward the paper as we hear another bell toll.)

PENDLETON: Oh, okay—I get it. It's the paper you've written your review of my life in, isn't it?

(C C Y C smiles. Motions toward the paper, another bell toll.)

PENDLETON: Okay, fine! But what exactly is the point in my reading it now? I promise you that from this point on…

(C C Y C *motions toward the paper again, a loud thunderclap as* PENDLETON *jumps, frightened.*)

PENDLETON: Fine! I get it! I get it! (*He hurries over to the paper, tentatively takes hold of it and sits at the foot of the bed. He starts looking through it, noticing there is nothing near the front pages. He looks over at* C C Y C.) Really? You couldn't put it at least in the front section? I'm not saying front page, but…

(C C Y C *points, ominous bell toll.*)

PENDLETON: Okay! Okay! (*He keeps looking for the review, moving all the way to the back section of the paper. He finally sees it, buried on the last page. He looks resentfully toward* C C Y C, *then starts to read:*) "The life of Hugh Pendleton." (*To* C C Y C) Well, ya got the spelling right, that's something I guess.

(C C Y C *points quickly.*)

PENDLETON: Okay, okay, no more thunder, please— I'm in a very fragile place right now. (*Back to reading*) "While first showing exceptional promise…" (*Turns to* C C Y C) Hey, not so bad—I've had worse, trust me. "Exceptional" could even be a pull quote. (*Back to reading*) "Mr Pendleton's meteoric—DESCENT?" Wow, really? (*Reading to himself now*) Ouch. Holy— wow. Cripes, you really went personal.

(C C Y C *smiles with pride.* PENDLETON *continues reading, holding the paper at a distance, hardly able to take it anymore. He finally stops, looks over at* C C Y C, *tossing the paper on the bed.*)

PENDLETON: Alright, that's enough. worst review in the history of time, I get it.

(C C Y C starts to leave again. PENDLETON *gets off the bed, goes to stop him.)*

PENDLETON: Wait, wait, wait—where are you going?

(CCYC stops, stands across from PENDLETON.*)*

PENDLETON: Look, that's the review, but what's the verdict? Am I to close early? Or will I get to extend my run?

(C C Y C just glares at PENDLETON.*)*

PENDLETON: Well? Is it thumbs up? Or thumbs down?

(C C Y C slowly extends his hand out, with only his thumb sticking out. He holds it there, sideways for a moment. He seems to love torturing PENDLETON.*)*

PENDLETON: Well?!

(C C Y C gives PENDLETON *the "Thumbs down". All at once, a cacophony of noise, chimes, wind, an awful din drowning* PENDLETON *out as he looks up toward the heavens and screams:)*

PENDLETON: Nooooooooooooooo!!!!!

(As C C Y C *disappears and* PENDLETON *starts to spin around, as though caught in an invisible vortex that sucks him toward the back of the set. He spins in circles, finally moving through the split in the center of the curtain as just before he goes through, the lights bump to black. As they come up again, we see the set is empty, the sounds have faded and the light is different, brighter, as it is a new day.)*

(Over, we hear the sound of snoring coming from backstage. It's interrupted by horrible singing. Someone is singing a current obnoxious [pick one], and loud, pop song, as a JANITOR enters from the back of the house, perhaps with ear buds in his ears. Suddenly the snoring stops, and PENDLETON's face appears poking through the curtain, toward the house. He calls to the janitor.

PENDLETON: Hey, you there!?

(The JANITOR *continues to sing, loudly and awfully, as* PENDLETON *tries again:)*

PENDLETON: Hey, HELLO!

(The JANITOR *is startled, quickly takes his ear buds out, looks to* PENDLETON.*)*

JANITOR: Whoa, man, geez, did ya have to freak me out like that? Ya almost gave me a coronary.

*(*PENDLETON *walks through the curtain, heads downstage.)*

PENDLETON: Are you another spirit? Wait, that would be four. Since when are there four spirits?

JANITOR: Uh, no, I'm a janitor. See, it says "janitor" — here on my shirt. And I'm holding a mop. How much more like a janitor can I look?

PENDLETON: What is today?

JANITOR: It's Christmas day, man.

PENDLETON: Are you sure?

JANITOR: What, you think janitors are stupid? That we don't know what day it is?

PENDLETON: *(To self)* All in one night! They did it all in one night! And wait, why are you working today. It's Christmas.

JANITOR: I'm a Jew, dude. Is that okay? Because I know it isn't okay for a lot of people.

PENDLETON: Of course, of course—that's totally fine.

JANITOR: Wow, I'm so relieved, thank you.

PENDLETON: You are most welcome, sir! *(Does little jig)* Oh, I'm as giddy as a summer apprentice, as care free as a theatre major before the loans kick in.

JANITOR: Well, that's great man, but if you don't mind, I have to get back to work here.

PENDLETON: My fine fellow, do you know the A & P on the corner?

JANITOR: Who doesn't know the A & P?

PENDLETON: There's a fish section in back.

(PENDLETON *burrows in his pocket, has a couple bills, presses them in the* JANITOR's *hand.*)

PENDLETON: Take this, go quickly and buy me the biggest halibut they have.

JANITOR: Why?

PENDLETON: Oh, I don't know—just for the "halibut." *(Laughs at himself)* See what I did there?

JANITOR: Afraid so, yeah.

PENDLETON: Get a whole fish, with the head, and deliver it to 10 Woodland Road. Wrapped in suitable paper of course.

JANITOR: Mind if I ask you something first?

PENDLETON: Of course, fine lad.

JANITOR: Why do you think it's okay to ask someone you just met to do an errand for you? You don't find that a little presumptuous at all?

PENDLETON: Off with you, lad! No more dawdling, I have much to do!

JANITOR: Fine, but stop calling me "lad," I'm fifty-three years old, dude.

PENDLETON: Go!

JANITOR: *(Noticing money* PENDLETON *gave him)* Wait, this isn't even real money. This is prop money, man.

PENDLETON: No matter! Off with you! Go!

(Confused, the JANITOR *wanders off, putting his ear buds back in.)*

PENDLETON: *(To self)* Oh, what a delightful Jewish person. A fantastical Jewish person! *(Walks up stage)* Oh, how insensitive of me I should have wished him a happy *(Severely mispronounced)* "Chanuka".

(Suddenly GEORGE sticks his head through the backdrop from backstage, sees his uncle. He steps through.)

GEORGE: Uncle Hugh?

(PENDLETON runs over to GEORGE, lifts him up, hugs him.)

PENDLETON: George! My dear nephew!

GEORGE: Uhm, wow—okay uhm—what are you still doing here? I just came to check on the windows. The one in back is broken and it's snowing pretty hard out there.

PENDLETON: Snowing!? How wonderful, on this glorious Christmas Day!

GEORGE: Are you okay? The last time we talked…

PENDLETON: I know, George—I'm a pigheaded old fool. I was rude, and ungrateful and I was wrong.

GEORGE: Oh—kay.

(TINA steps out from behind the backdrop.)

TINA: *(To GEORGE)* Did he just admit he was wrong?

PENDLETON: I most certainly did young lady.

TINA: Are you drunk again?

GEORGE: Tina!

PENDLETON: No, no, no, the lady asks a fair question. And I'm proud to say that at the present time, while quite hung over, I am most certainly not drunk. I want to say how sorry I am. To both of you. I've been misguided, selfish and rude—especially to you Tina, and for that I offer my most sincere apology.

GEORGE: WOW—this is wow.

TINA: What's the catch?

PENDLETON: No catch. I've been reminded what a special vocation this is. What a gift it is to work in this profession. I understand that more than ever now. And I want you to know that if you'll both have me—I would be thrilled—no, honored, to come back next season. I'd especially like to give ol' Ebenezer another go. I feel I understand him more than ever now.

GEORGE: Well, this is very surprising, to say the least.

TINA: It is.

PENDLETON: All I ask is that you consider it.

TINA: Yeah, we'll get back to you on that. Come on, George.

(TINA *starts out,* GEORGE *hesitates.*)

GEORGE: *(To* TINA*)* All due respect dearest, I'm going to have to override you on this one. *(Looks at his uncle)* I'd be thrilled to have you back, Uncle.

TINA: Are you insane?

GEORGE: I'm sure I am.

(TINA *squirms, swallows the idea.*)

TINA: Fine, but no more Beckham plays.

PENDLETON: I promise we won't produce one single play by David Beckham.

TINA: *(A huge victory)* Thank you.

GEORGE: Please, come back to our place for leftovers. We've got lots.

PENDLETON: I would love that. I'll just gather up my things.

GEORGE: Alright, then, see you soon, Uncle. *(He starts out.)*

PENDLETON: Oh, George?

(GEORGE *stops.*)

GEORGE: Yes, Uncle?

PENDLETON: You remind me so much of your mother.

GEORGE: *(Very moved)* Well, thank you. And Merry Christmas.

PENDLETON: Merry Christmas.

(GEORGE *heads backstage.* TINA *just stands there, suspicious.* PENDLETON *looks at her.*)

PENDLETON: And of course a Merry Christmas to you as well, Tina.

(TINA *starts to head out, then turns around.*)

TINA: If you want coffee, bring some half and half. We ran out.

PENDLETON: I'd be delighted. Low fat, or…

TINA: Whatevs.

PENDLETON: "Whatevs" it will be.

(TINA *exits.* DEREK *appears at the back of the house, holding Mr Marple's carrier in one hand, and something wrapped in dripping wet brown paper in the other.*)

DEREK: Mr Pendleton?

PENDLETON: *(Sees him)* Sedgwick!

DEREK: Derek actually.

PENDLETON: Right, of course.

DEREK: Mr Pendleton, a kind of strange janitor type person delivered this very large fish to my apartment and told me you were the one who sent it. And I'm just kind of uhm, a little confused. Why did you send this? It smells and it's dripping and so totally beyond gross.

PENDLETON: Well, it was meant for Mr Carpels, of course.

DEREK: Marples, actually.

PENDLETON: Right, Marples.

DEREK: Yeah, but how would I even feed it to him? *(Tries)* See, it wouldn't even fit in his carrier.

(PENDLETON *pauses for a moment, then pulls up one of the chairs.)*

PENDLETON: Young man, have a seat. I feel the need to communicate something to you.

DEREK: Are you gonna communicate like you did yesterday? Because that was really mean.

PENDLETON: At last night's show alone you missed by my count, three lighting cues, you never hung my robe up in the same place twice and my makeup mirror was almost entirely covered in smudges. I'm simply not going to take it any more. You sir, are hired.

DEREK: Wait, what?

PENDLETON: You heard me. You're hired.

DEREK: I'm sorry, I think my ears are—I thought you said "hired"?

PENDLETON: I did. I will see to it that you are taken on as a full member of the company. And I'll make sure you have plenty of small roles to start honing your craft.

DEREK: You mean like—as an actor?

PENDLETON: No, I mean like—as a dentist. Yes, as an actor.

DEREK: But—but…

PENDLETON: What do ya say—will you join our company?

DEREK: I'd be honored, sir.

PENDLETON: Great. Merry Christmas, (*Struggling at first, then:*) —Derek!

(DEREK *inhales, shocked to hear his actual name.* PENDLETON *looks toward the carrier. Even putting a finger near the cage*)

PENDLETON: And happy kitty Christmas to you too, you adorable little pussy puss.

(*Mr Marples screeches angrily, almost biting him.* PENDLETON *pulls his hand back, trying to keep from backhanding the cage. Under his breath:*)

PENDLETON: Mangy little dust bag.

DEREK: And Merry Christmas to you, Mr Pendleton!

(GEORGE *and* TINA *come out from backstage. He addresses the audience.*)

GEORGE: And indeed my uncle was even better than his word. Our little theatre thrived, audiences flocked and even critics were—well, they were mixed, but whatever.

(*They all respond with "whatever" shrugs regarding critics.*)

TINA: And to Derek and Mr Marples, who lived, stopped frothing at the mouth and only had to have one paw amputated because of cat diabetes—Hugh Pendleton was a second father.

DEREK: And ever afterwards it was said of Hugh Pendleton that he knew how to keep theatre in his heart.

TINA: But most importantly, to keep *A Christmas Carol* up and running, so as to make up for all the other disastrous programming choices we made that hemorrhaged money and that no one wanted to see anyway.

PENDLETON: And so from our little company to yours:

(All together)

DEREK/GEORGE/PENDLETON/TINA: God Bless us all—
everyone!

*(DEREK holds up Mr Marple's cage. We hear several distinct
and celebratory meows.)*

DEREK/GEORGE/PENDLETON/TINA: And a Happy New
Year!

(As The Wassail Song *plays again, and the cast leads
everyone in a sing along and an atmosphere of general
frivolity ensues.)*

END OF PLAY

Lightning Source UK Ltd.
Milton Keynes UK
UKHW021142071020
371159UK00006B/293